MW00388138

El Morro
National Monument

El Morro is a cuesta—a rock formation that gently slopes upward and then abruptly drops off. Winds, desert streams, and ancient seas created the singular geology of this sandstone rock face. The prominent, long vertical "joints" are the result of shifting plates pushing from below and now-eroded rock pushing from above, cracking the sandstone during many thousands of years.

One of the significant documents of southwestern history is a rock. "El Morro," the great rock with its hidden waterhole, was the tablet where the First People carved their symbols. Later, Spanish conquistadores found it and carved their own names. Eventually Americans following the desert trail added their own marks. Today the ancient tablet bears the marks, names, and sometimes the hopes, of hundreds of people of at least three cultures.

A rock is not as "easy" a document as parchment in an archive. To understand the cryptic names and symbols often requires help from the scholars in the library. But the names on the rock have another value. Most citizens never see original historic documents. They may know what an explorer's letter home said, but they rarely get to see the letter itself. Part of the magic of El Morro is that the modern visitor stands in the same sand and sunshine as the traveler long ago and can almost hear the scrape of a knife slowly carving letters in the sandstone. It is a rare point of contact that reaches across centuries.

It all began with the waterhole. The pool in the shadow of El Morro was an Eden for desert travelers who found it. Snowmelt and rain coming off the rock filled the pool. The rock shaded it from the desert's fierce evaporation, so the pool was reliable—the only reliable water for thirty miles in either direction, and the only water on the old route between the pueblos of Acoma and Zuni. Early accounts, and the existence of petroglyphs where the water now laps against the rock, tell us that the pool used to be surrounded by a grassy sandbank. Later, men enlarged the pool, but from the beginning it contained water. Only one whose mouth has been parched can know what that can mean on the desert.

The First People

On top of the great rock is a roughly rectangular mound. Its shape and occasional broken pieces of pottery washing out at its base tell the knowledgeable observer that this mound is actually a prehistoric Indian village of more than five hundred rooms. Years of archeological work in the area tell us much of the Indians' story. Before they built the village at the top of the rock, they lived scattered through the valley, slowly adopting the ways of agriculture, learning new techniques in making pottery, and new ways of building homes. Several of these early, scattered dwellings are nearby. Then, around A.D. 1200, something happened. We still don't know exactly why it was, but people began to leave their small, scattered villages and gather into large, pre-planned towns—places like A'ts'ina, the dwelling on top of El Morro.

In the late 1950s two Chevrolet Carryalls appeared at the foot of the cliff, carrying archeologists Dick and Nathalie Woodbury. (The Zuni workmen soon nicknamed Mrs. Woodbury *"Sho-ma-kolo-wa,"* or "Dragonfly," from watching her carry lunch to them up the mesa. In her bright red top she may have looked slightly like one, but also there are Zuni stories in which a dragonfly brings food.) Sleeping in the Carryalls, cooking on a Coleman stove under a canvas fly, heating water for washing by putting filled jerry cans in the sun, the archeologists began to unravel the story of the town on top of the mesa. The 'dig' determined that a small, previous village had been dismantled and its stones used for the new one. Tree-ring dates revealed that around A.D. 1275 the ancient builders began the large, pre-planned town. Its square plaza was surrounded by a double line of single-story rooms, and outside that, a double line of two-story rooms. The outside presented a blank wall with access via ladders. Many archeologists believe the town, like others built in the valley about the same time, was defensive. For perhaps two generations the town thrived, and one guesses the people of A'ts'ina may have been envied for their reliable water supply in the hidden pool at the base of the cliff.

These people, and probably also the people living in the scattered villages before them, were first to carve on the rock we call El Morro. You can see

Evidence of those who have passed El Morro stretch back to prehistoric times, when the ancestral Pueblo people left their inscriptions in the form of petroglyphs. These marks are created by engraving, carving, or pecking away the dark layer of varnish on a rock's surface to reveal the lighter rock underneath.

their marks—petroglyphs—today, weather-worn from hundreds of winters: animal-like figures, little 'stick-men,' swirling geometric forms. Most are beyond our understanding today. They try to speak across the centuries, but the words, even the thoughts, are lost. Their makers did not merely speak a different language from ours but were people in a different world, a culture different to its very roots. We know that in many ways they were like us. Certainly they needed the water from the pool, and they needed and built shelter. But these petroglyphs hint at gods and fears and even laughter very different from our own. A few we can know at least in part. The present-day Pueblo Indians are descendants of the people who carved them and sometimes a Pueblo will recognize a god who still dances in the great ceremonies. But most petroglyphs remain tantalizing images from the people who first used the pool at El Morro.

The Spaniards

The ancestral Puebloans had long left the village at the top of the rock and established the nearby pueblos of Zuni and Acoma when almost unbelievable tales began to filter in. Somewhere to the south there were people of a different color with fantastic technology. One must think of modern tales of people from Mars to understand the shock. The newcomers came equipped with animals they could ride at great speed. No Indian, whose domestic animals were turkeys and dogs, had ever heard of such a thing. The newcomers had metal weapons—another new concept. Soon there was proof of the unbelievable, as Spaniards coming up from what is now old Mexico entered the region, and every Indian saw the newcomers for himself. Thus began the rich, beautiful, sometimes rancorous cultural mix that became even more complicated with the addition of Anglos a few centuries later.

The first foreign expedition we are sure reached the great rock and its precious pool was that of Antonio de Espejo. On March 11, 1583, their journal records that they camped at *"El Estanque del Peñol"*—"The Pool by the Great Rock." El Morro, not yet so named, had entered into written history. The Spanish explorers did not carve their names on it, though, or if they did the inscription has not been discovered.

Don Juan de Oñate (1605)

The oldest non-Indian inscription on the rock contains one of the great names in the history of the Southwest. After various explorations, Spanish authorities in what is today's Mexico decided to colonize the lands to the north. In 1598 the illustrious Don Juan de Oñate, with close to a thousand fellow settlers and 7,000 head of livestock, came plodding north and planted the first Spanish settlement in what is now the southwestern United States, near present-day Santa Fe. That same year he visited El Morro (calling it

TOP: Petroglyphs at El Morro record the natural world as well as the spiritual.
BOTTOM: Ramon Garcia Jurado inscription, carved in 1709.

"Agua de la Peña"–Water of the Rock). He did not carve the inscription we see today on that trip, but we do know something about the visit. One of his men was especially glad to find the waterhole. Gaspar Pérez de Villagrá, who later would write one of the great accounts of the period, became separated from the expedition, lost, and was thrown from his horse. Wandering, near death, he chanced on El Morro. He wrote, "At last I arrived at a great cliff at whose foot flowed a crystalline stream. I threw myself into its water, blinded and burning with thirst, and drank long of its cool waters"

"At last I arrived at a great cliff at whose foot flowed a crystalline stream. I threw myself into its waters, blinded and burning with thirst, and drank long its cool waters."

Six years later, in 1604, Governor Oñate led another expedition to the Gulf of California, which he called the "South Sea." Coming back, he camped by the now familiar waterhole on April 15, 1605, and with that visit the rock became a modern history book.

On a spring morning fifteen years before the Pilgrims landed at Plymouth Rock, Oñate or someone in his group carved on the rock the synopsis of his expedition:

"Paso por aq(u)i el adelantado don Juan de Oñate del descubrimiento del Mar del Sur el 16 de abril de 1605."

"Here passed by the Governor-General Don Juan de Oñate, from the discovery of the South Sea, the 16th of April, 1605."

The phrase *"Paso por aqui"*—"He passed by here"—captures the spirit of El Morro. It appears repeatedly on the rock and has made its way into the title of numerous articles and books.

One wonders if Oñate ever thought about that lone inscription on the rock by the pool in later years. His fledgling colony in disarray, his own fortune sunk in it and lost, Oñate returned to Mexico and more political troubles. Nevertheless, he had left his mark in the new land.

Governor Don Juan de Eulate(?) (1620)(?)

Another early Spanish inscription is fascinating for the personality it reveals. Unfortunately, reading rocks is an uncertain business, and subsequent damage makes it unclear who did the carving, or when. One of the longest on the rock reads:

"Soy Capitan-General de las provincias del Nuevo Mexico por el Rey nuestro Senor. Paso por aqui de buelta de los pueblos de Zuñi a los 29 de Julio ano de 1620(?) y los puso en pas a su pedimiento pidiendole su favor como basallos de su magistad y de nuebo dieron la obediencia todo lo que hiso con el agasaxo selo y prudencia como tan christianisimo [XXXXXX] tan particular y gallardo soldado de inacabable y loada mem [XXXXXX]."

"I am the captain General of the Providences of New Mexico for the

King our Lord, passed by here on the return from the pueblos of Zuni on the 29th of July the year 1620, and put them at peace at their humble petition, they asking favor as vassals of his Majesty and promising anew their obedience, all of which he did, with clemency, zeal, and prudence, as a most Christian-like (gentleman) extraordinary and gallant soldier of enduring and praised memory."

This may have been Governor Eulate but the carving is not clear so we are uncertain. Whoever it was, his opinion of himself and his accomplishments was not shared by all. Some of the obliterations were deliberate, and there are scratches on the inscription as though someone objected to it. The erasures are early; they appear on a copy made in 1849.

Letrado and Luján (1632)

Spain was tempted to withdraw from New Mexico after Oñate's problems, but the Franciscan priests, who had begun a missionary effort, persuaded the Crown to stay. Thus during the 1600s the colony was essentially a missionary effort. One missionary was Fray Francisco Letrado. He came from Mexico in 1629 and was stationed at the Salinas Province, east of the Rio Grande. Transferred to Zuni in 1632, he had been at his new post just a few weeks when he was killed by the Zunis on February 22, 1632. Word must have reached Santa Fe very quickly, to judge from the inscription

> "Se pasaron a 23 de Marzo de 1632 anos a la benganza de muerte del Padre Letrado. Luján."
>
> "They passed on March 23, 1632, to the avenging of the death of Father Letrado. Luján."

Luján, presumably the soldier who did the carving, was quite efficient. He used a sort of shorthand, with some letters deliberately missing, probably due to the difficulty of carving. We have no record of what happened when the soldiers arrived at Zuni.

Don Francisco Manuel de Silva Nieto (1629)

In 1629 someone carved the only poem on the rock. In summer of that year, Governor Manuel de Silva Nieto journeyed west to station new priests at Acoma, Zuni, and Hopi. His party stopped for rest and water at the pool, and during the visit Governor Nieto or one of his men carved the eulogy. Parts are obliterated, but it reads:

> "Aqui [XXXXXX] y Governado Don Francisco Manuel de Silva Nieto Que lo ynposible tiene ya sujeto Su Braco yndubitable y su Balor Conlos carros

Travelers along ancient trade routes depended on El Morro's water, a pool of rain runoff and snowmelt. In the shade of the bluff, it provided much-needed relief from grueling desert conditions.

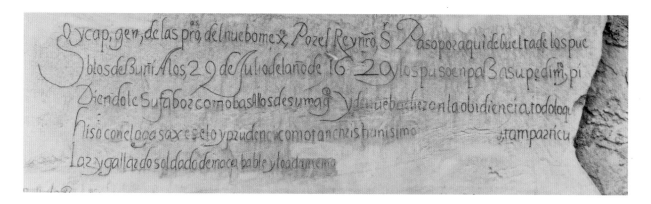

Circumstances for Revolt

Relations with the pueblos were determined mainly through the *encomienda* system, in which ranking citizens *(encomenderos)* were appointed by the governor to provide protection, aid, and education to Indians and military support for the government in return for the privilege of collecting tribute. But the system was abused, and New Mexico was too remote for the exploitation to be checked by higher authorities. The Franciscans tried to lighten the burden on the Indians, but the settlers and government refused to give up the profitable arrangement, and in any case, the friars themselves placed heavy demands on the pueblos to support the missions.

Drought, widespread famine, and more than a century of mistreatment decimated the Indian population of New Mexico. The ability of the pueblos to withstand these disasters may have been lessened by the disruption of their culture under Spanish rule. In August 1680 the northern pueblos, in an uncharacteristic show of unity, revolted and expelled the Spaniards from New Mexico.

del Rei Nuestro Senor Cosa quesolo el Puso en este Efecto, De Agosto 5 seiscientos Beinte y Nueve Que se bien a Zuñi pasa y la Fe lleve."

In English it does not rhyme:

"Here passed I the Governor Francisco Manuel de Silva Nieto Who has done the impossible, by his invincible arm and his valor, with the wagons of the King our Master, a thing to which he alone put into effect August 5, 1629, that one may pass to Zuni and carry the faith."

Other records indicate that Governor Nieto indeed took wagons across that route. A look at the countryside confirms that it certainly was an achievement.

Diego de Vargas (1692)

Though short, the Vargas inscription represents a tumultuous decade. Throughout the 1600s, the period of the missions, there was tension between the governors and the priests. Caught between cross and crown, forced to support both, near the end of the century the Indians' bitterness boiled over. On August 10, 1680, they revolted. Four hundred Spaniards were killed and the terrified remnant straggled down the Rio Grande. For twelve years New Mexico was Indian again.

The man who eventually succeeded in reconquest bore the formidable name Diego José de Vargas Zapata y Lujan Ponce de León y Contreras. (He did not put it all on the rock.) In 1692 Diego de Vargas led his small army of three hundred north. They approached Santa Fe in September, and by boldly walking in with the assumption of victory, took the city without a fight. It happened over and over as Vargas toured the territory. He would approach a pueblo, which undoubtedly had already heard that the pueblo before them had capitulated, and offer blood or peace. The pueblos surrendered. He visited pueblos north, east, and south of Santa Fe, with the same results. Finally he swung west. Zuni rejoined the Spanish flag, and a few days later, Vargas and his men stopped at El Morro for water. It is in Vargas' journal that the term "El Morro" appears, Spanish for a headland, or cliff, particularly one looming over a sea. The Vargas inscription reads:

"Aqui estubo el General Don Diego de Vargas, quien conquisto a nuestra Santa Fe y a la Real Corona todo el Nuebo Mexico a su costa, Año de 1692."

"Here was the General Don Diego de Vargas, who conquered to our Holy Faith and to the Royal Crown, all of New Mexico at his own expense, year of 1692."

The peace did not last. When Vargas brought new colonists to the re-conquered kingdom, rebellion broke out. Vargas used the sword to put it down. Vargas was a truly remarkable man, conciliatory or warlike in turn, who sometimes seemed by sheer force of personality to settle very tense situations. But recent research shows another side to him, too. His letters home reveal a man lonely for his family, worried about finances, concerned about family land in Spain, homesick, and anxious for honors that never came. He had political troubles, lost the governorship, and then regained it. Still a privately troubled man, far from home, in 1704 he became sick while leading a campaign against Apaches and died near present-day Bernalillo, New Mexico. His legacy, some say, is the continued existence of Spanish influence in the American Southwest; but the only actual physical marks of his you can see today are the words scratched into the rock at El Morro.

General Hurtado and Corporal Truxillo (1736)

Juan Páez Hurtado, who had been with Vargas through the emotion-filled days of the reconquest, was Vargas' lieutenant governor for a time and even governor in 1705, after Vargas' death. Now, thirty years later, the colony was comparatively quiet. The law required biennial inspections of the pueblos, probably the occasion for this trip:

"El dia 14 de Julio de 1736 Paso por aque el General Juan Paez Hurtado, Visitador."

"The 14th of July of 1736 passed by here the General Juan Páez Hurtado, Inspector."

But not only great men came to El Morro; lesser men get thirsty too. Below this inscription, in another hand but obviously meant to be connected to it, was added:

TOP LEFT: Governor Don Juan de Eulate may have carved this inscription on the rock in 1620.
BELOW: Luján, probably a soldier, carved this message in March 1632.

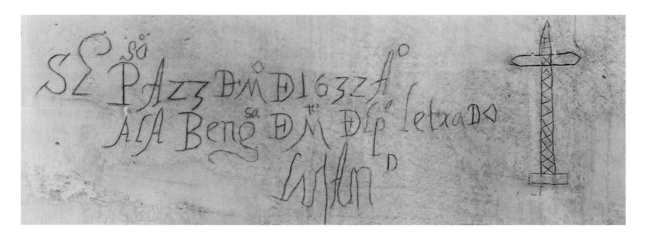

The people of A'ts'ina may have been envied for their reliable water supply in the hidden pool at the base of the cliff.

*"y en su compania el Cabo, Joseph
Truxillo."*

"and in his company the Corporal, Joseph
Truxillo."

("Cabo" can also mean "leader," not specifically
the rank as we know it.)

The inscription is on the north side of the rock
out of sight of the pool.

Sometime during the visit, Hurtado found a
blank space on the rock and carved his message
with his dagger. Later Corporal Truxillo found the
new inscription and entered his own name in the
Southwest's most permanent history book. The
ordinary men of the world salute you, Corporal
Joseph Truxillo.

Martin de Elizacochea, Bishop of Durango (1737)

The year after Inspector Hurtado and his corporal camped at the pool, the
Bishop of Durango visited the northern missions:

*"Dia 28 de Septiembre de 1737 años llego aqui El Illustrisimo Señor Doctor
Don Martin de Elizacochea, Obispo de Durango y el dio 29 paso a Zuñi."*

"The 28th of September of 1737 arrived here the most illustrious
Senor Doctor Don Martin de Elizacochea, Bishop of Durango, and
the 29th passed to Zuni."

The Bishop had his own corporal, for on the other side of the rock is
another inscription:

*"El dia 29 de Septiembre de 1737 anos llego aqui el Bachiller Don Juan
Ignacio de Arrasain."*

"The 28th of September of 1737, arrived here the Bachelor Don Juan
Ignacio de Arrasain."

Arrasain was secretary to the Bishop of Durango. "Bachelor" indicates a
"Bachelor of Laws" degree. These two carvings are in the same hand. Likely
the Bishop had his secretary do the carving.

We know the setting of the visit by the Bishop of Durango, but unfortunately not the particulars of this visit. The Franciscans in New Mexico claimed
to be beyond the jurisdiction of the Bishop of Durango, whose authority
had been defined loosely: "...to the North Sea." The Bishop claimed jurisdiction over New Mexico and reenforced his claim when the refugees from
the revolt settled in El Paso in the 1680s, definitely in his realm. In 1733 the
Viceroy in Mexico upheld the Bishop's claim, and the next higher authority,
the Council of the Indies, agreed in 1738. This inscription shows that even
before that confirmation, the Bishop had ventured far north to the deserts of
New Mexico to visit his flock, and along the way rested at the pool by the rock.

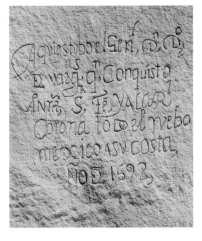

LEFT AND TOP: A'ts'ina, atop
El Morro, dates from about A.D. 1275
and was inhabited for two generations. The Zuni, ancestors of those
who lived there, regard it as sacred.
BOTTOM: Formidably named Diego
José de Vargas Zapata y Lujan
Ponce de León y Contreras recorded
his visit to El Morro after recon-
quering Zuni and other pueblos for
the Spanish crown in 1692.

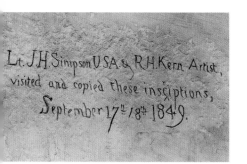

First Lieutenant James Harvey Simpson of the Corps of Topographical Engineers, U.S. Army, and artist Richard H. Kern passed by El Morro as part of the U.S. Army's exploration of its new territories after the U.S.-Mexican War.

Saving the Monument

The lands surrounding Inscription Rock were reserved from settlement or entry by order of the Secretary of the Interior June 14, 1901, and on December 8, 1906, shortly after the passage of the Antiquities Act, El Morro National Monument was created. June 18, 1917, the monument was enlarged to 240 acres by the addition of 80 acres containing ruins of archeological interest. Today the park area covers more than 1,200 acres.

The last dated Spanish inscription on the rock is from 1774:

"Por aqui paso Andres Romero."

We know nothing of Andrés Romero, save this: He was a man somehow making a living in the remote Spanish colony of New Mexico; he was on a difficult journey and undoubtedly knew thirst. He found rest at the pool at El Morro and he had the same impulse as the great and ordinary before him, to make his name immortal on the rock. For at least a millennium the land and the rock and its pool, had belonged to Indians. Then for two centuries Spain had explored, lost, reconquered, settled, and crisscrossed the land. For more than twenty years it was Mexican, after that country had succeeded in its revolt against Spain, though there are no inscriptions clearly from the Mexican Period (1821-1846). Now would come the time of the Americans.

The Americans Arrive

In 1846 the energies of the young United States of America spilled over. The War with Mexico began, and down the Santa Fe Trail came the Army of the West under General Stephen Watts Kearny. Two years later it was over and El Morro—plus present-day Texas, New Mexico, southern California, and most of Arizona—changed hands. The United States lost no time consolidating its hold on the new territories. In those days, it was customary for artists to accompany army exploration and cartographic parties:

"Lt. J.H. Simpson USA and R.H. Kern, Artist, visited and copied these inscriptions, September 17th 18th, 1849."

First Lieutenant James Harvey Simpson of the Corps of Topographical Engineers, U.S. Army, and the Philadelphia artist Richard H. Kern had been guided to El Morro by a Mr. Lewis, Navajo trader, who told them about "half an acre of inscriptions on a rock." They spent two days at El Morro copying inscriptions. It is Kern's drawing that proves the obliterations on the Eulate(?) inscription were there by 1849. Kern saw much of the West during his work as an artist. He was with an army unit that explored the Pecos River in 1850; that fall he traveled across northern Arizona with Lt. Lorenzo Sitgreaves and again added his name to El Morro; he finally was killed by Indians in central Utah on October 26, 1853.

Beale (1859)

Surely the strangest sight at El Morro was in 1857. The United States Army decided on a remarkable experiment. They would try camels. After purchasing some in Egypt and attempting to train both the camels and their army handlers in Texas, a test trip was set up across the Southwest. The commander was Lt. Edward Fitzgerald Beale, formerly of the U.S. Navy but now in the Department of Indian Affairs. The man in charge of the camels was P. Gilmer Breckinridge. In addition to experimenting with camels, they pioneered a new route to California. They first stopped at El Morro on August 23, 1857, though there is evidence that they carved their names on a subsequent visit in 1859.

Although the camels did well, the experiment did not lead to use of camels by the military. There were problems, mostly in the reaction of army horses—and teamsters—to the unfamiliar animals. Then the advent of the Civil War ended the experiment, and after the war the rapid expansion of the railroads eliminated the need. The camels were sold or released. For decades tales circulated of sightings of camels on the desert, and some may have been true.

The First Emigrant Wagon Train

Twenty-six Anglo names appear on the cliff with the dates of July 7 or 8, 1858. This was the first emigrant train to use this trail to the West Coast. Even told briefly, the story indicates that behind these twenty-six names is an intensity of experience, of ambition and sorrow, and of pain.

Visitors to El Morro enjoy hiking, picnicking, camping, and a fascinating look at one of the Southwest's best records of the many cultures that have passed through New Mexico.

The wagon train had left Missouri in early April, 1858, its members bound for new lives in the Eden of California. Fearing conflict between the U.S. Army and the Mormons in Utah that summer, they chose the southern route, following the old Santa Fe Trail to Albuquerque. There is a world of experience in that phrase, "following the old Santa Fe Trail:" storms, the broad prairies, the intoxicating exhilaration of buffalo hunts, even the mundane details of prairie travel. One man got in trouble with his wife for hunting buffalo on a Sunday! In Albuquerque they somehow fell in with the man who had guided Beale's camel expedition the year before. They decided to follow the new route and hired him. This is what brought them to camp at the pool of El Morro on July 7.

Leaving their names carved in the rock, they pushed on. Near present-day Flagstaff, they acted like tourists everywhere, marvelling at the view and rolling boulders off the cliffs. But from just west of there the trouble began. They lost their way often and sometimes could not find water—they must have remembered the pool at El Morro. They also began to encounter Indians. Mojaves came into camp to beg, but when they left the emigrants found that cattle had been stolen. Perhaps more experienced frontiersmen could have reversed the situation, but this group didn't. They straggled, and one whole family was killed when they foolishly separated from the group. When the train finally reached the Colorado River at the present Arizona-California border, they had a full-scale battle with the Indians. Barricaded behind the wagons, they took a heavy toll in Indian lives while losing few men themselves. Nevertheless, they could not prevent the Indians driving off almost all their cattle and horses.

Surely the strangest sight at El Morro was in 1857. The United States Army decided on a remarkable experiment. They would try camels. After purchasing some in Egypt and attempting to train both camels and army handlers in Texas, a test trip set out across the Southwest.

Now they were afoot in strange country, on the California-Arizona border. Considering their options, they decided to turn back to Albuquerque, a mere six-hundred-mile walk through largely uninhabited desert. One journal says that John Udell carried his wife part way; the inscription on El Morro tells us he was 63 at the time. The journals don't tell us, but the hungry, desperately exhausted crowd must have looked forward to the pool at El Morro as they approached it for a second time. Most of them made it to Albuquerque, and incredibly, most of them tried again for California the next year, and made it. They deserve to have their names remembered on the rock at El Morro.

The Railroad Doesn't Come

Numerous names, all carved in 1868, add "U.P.R." That was the year the Union Pacific Railroad sent a survey party past El Morro, planning to lay track on this venerable route to California. Instead, the Santa Fe built a line that passed about 20 miles north. The railroad revolutionized travel, and the centuries-long prominence of the pool at El Morro, and the great stone travelers' register, passed. Many whose hands had carved the rock were dead, some for centuries. Others, living in distant homesteads or stationed at army outposts, could remember refreshment at the hidden waterhole. But now it was in a backwater of the westward movement, yet holding another treasure: a record of the people who carved *"Paso por aqui"*—"They passed by here." The scholar learns much in the library, but here at the pool we can almost touch the people who rested here.

Other Places to Visit

Bandelier National Monument

Chaco Culture National Historical Park

El Malpais National Monument

Pecos National Historical Park

Petroglyph National Monument

Salinas Pueblo Missions National Monument

Further Reading

Kessell, John L. **Kiva, Cross & Crown.** Western National Parks Association, 1987.

Noble, David Grant, editor, and Richard B. Woodbury, editor. **Zuni and El Morro Past and Present.** Ancient City Press, 1993.

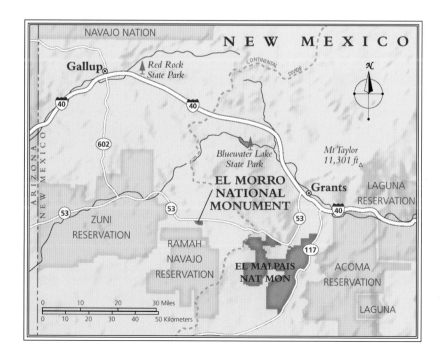

Copyright 2003 Western National Parks Association
Tucson, Arizona
Library of Congress number 88-063877
ISBN 1-58369-037-9
Written by Dan Murphy
Editorial: T.J. Priehs
Design: Melanie Doherty Design
Photography: Willard Clay, pg 14 (right); Bob and Suzanne Clemenz, pg 5
(top); Eliot Cohen, pg 5 (bottom), pg 11 (top); George A. Grant, courtesy NPS,
pg 8, 9, 11 (bottom), 12; George H. H. Huey, cover, pg 16; JC Leacock, pg 10,
14 (left); Morey K. Milbradt, pg 13; Jack Olson, pg 4; Tom Till, pg 2 and 7
Lithography: Printed in China

WESTERN
NATIONAL PARKS
ASSOCIATION

ISBN 1-58369-037-9
90000>

FOR $495

9 781583 690376